# ROMANIAN
## CHILDREN'S BOOK

### Learn Counting in Romanian by Coloring

## SIMONE SEAMS
— ILLUSTRATED BY DUY TRUONG —

# CONTENTS

# ONE
# Unu

# TWO

## Doi

# THREE
## Trei

# FOUR

## Patru

# FIVE

## Cinci

# SIX
## Șase

# SEVEN
## Șapte

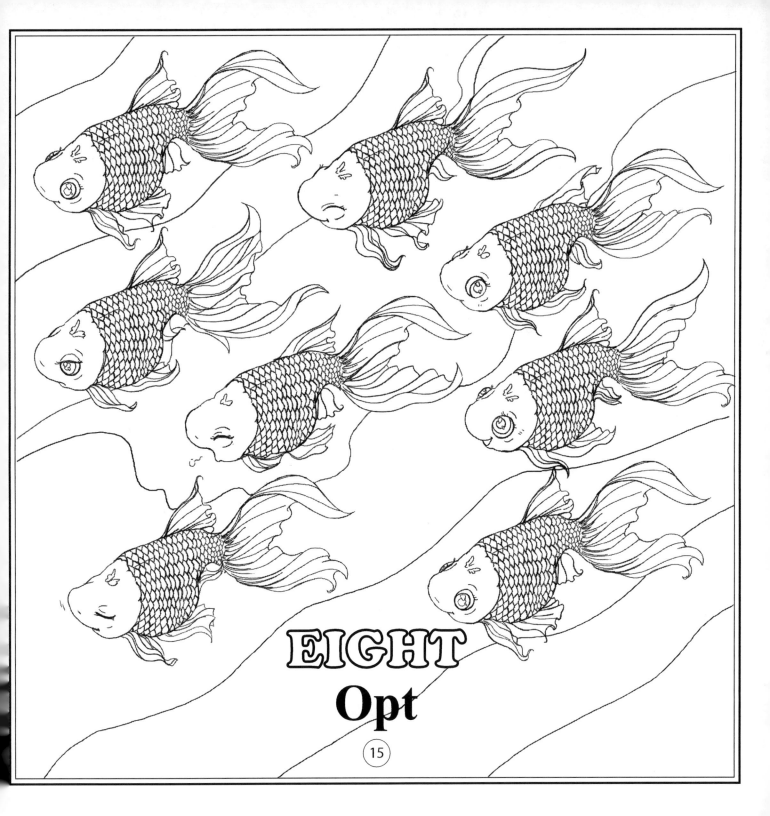

EIGHT
Opt

# NINE
## Nouă

# TEN
## Zece

# ELEVEN
## Unsprezece

# TWELVE
## Doisprezece

# THIRTEEN
## Treisprezece

# FOURTEEN
## Paisprezece

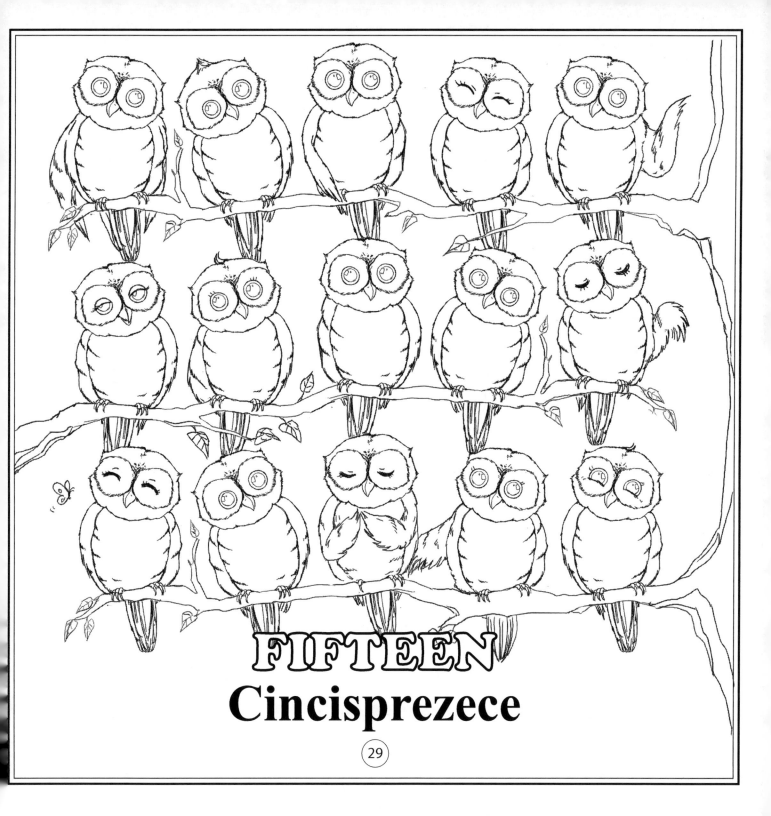

# FIFTEEN
## Cincisprezece

Made in the USA
Middletown, DE
21 February 2017